LAUGH -OUT- LOUD

JOKES FOR KIDS

THE BIG BOOK OF KNOCK-KNOCK JOKES

LAUGH -OUT- LOUD

JOKES FOR KIDS

THE BIG BOOK OF KNOCK-KNOCK JOKES

ROB ELLIOTT

HARPER

An Imprint of HarperCollinsPublishers

Library of Congress Control Number: 2021948141
ISBN 978-0-06-308066-9

21 22 23 24 25   PC/BRR   10 9 8 7 6 5 4 3 2 1
❖
First Edition

LAUGH
-OUT-
LOUD

JOKES FOR KIDS

THE BIG BOOK OF
KNOCK-KNOCK
JOKES

Table of Contents

- - - - - - - - - - - - - - - -

People

Knock, knock.

Who's there?

Juan.

Juan who?

You're Juan in a million!

Knock, knock.

Who's there?

Parker.

Parker who?

Parker bike in the garage.

Knock, knock.

Who's there?

Douglas.

Douglas who?

Douglas is empty, but I'm still thirsty.

Knock, knock.

Who's there?

Toby.

Toby who?

Toby or not to be, that is the question.

Knock, knock.

Who's there?

Turner.

Turner who?

Turner frown upside-down!

Knock, knock.

Who's there?

Homer.

Homer who?

You Homer should I come back later?

Knock, knock.

Who's there?

Aussie.

Aussie who?

Aussie your doorbell doesn't work!

Knock, knock.

Who's there?

Gus.

Gus who?

Gus what? I've got more knock-knock jokes for you!

Knock, knock.

Who's there?

Tom.

Tom who?

Tom for another knock-knock joke!

Knock, knock.

Who's there?

Wanda.

Wanda who?

**I Wanda if you'll ever answer the
door!**

Knock, knock.

Who's there?

Joanna.

Joanna who?

Joanna hear another knock-knock joke?

Knock, knock.

Who's there?

Amanda.

Amanda who?

Amanda fix the doorbell is here!

Knock, knock.

Who's there?

Heidi.

Heidi who?

Heidi key under the mat next time I come over!

Knock, knock.

Who's there?

Italian.

Italian who?

Italian your mother you won't open the door!

Knock, knock.

Who's there?

Philip.

Philip who?

Philip my glass with some water, please.

Knock, knock.

Who's there?

Sawyer.

Sawyer who?

Sawyer not going to let me in?

Knock, knock.

Who's there?

Olive.

Olive who?

Olive right down the street if you want to come over!

Knock, knock.

Who's there?

Irish.

Irish who?

Irish your doorbell worked because I'm sick of knocking!

Knock, knock.

Who's there?

Owen.

Owen who?

I was Owen you a visit so thought I'd stop by.

Knock, knock.

Who's there?

Megan.

Megan who?

Megan up a new knock-knock joke right now!

Knock, knock.

Who's there?

Oliver.

Oliver who?

Oliver jokes make me laugh!

Knock, knock.

Who's there?

Trish.

Trish who?

Yes, please. I have a runny nose.

Knock, knock.

Who's there?

Izzy.

Izzy who?

Izzy going to tell another knock-knock joke or not?

Knock, knock.

Who's there?

Lionel.

Lionel who?

A Lionel eat you if you're not careful!

Knock, knock.

Who's there?

Oswald.

Oswald who?

Oswald my bubble gum!

Knock, knock.

Who's there?

Wayne.

Wayne who?

The Wayne keeps falling, so open up!

Knock, knock.

Who's there?

Terri.

Terri who?

Terri goes again with those knock-
knock jokes!

Knock, knock.

Who's there?

Abel.

Abel who?

Abel would be a lot easier than
knocking!

Knock, knock.

Who's there?

Hugo.

Hugo who?

Hugo first and I'll follow!

Knock, knock.

Who's there?

Duncan.

Duncan who?

Duncan my cookies in a glass of milk.

Yum!

HA HA HA!

Knock, knock.

Who's there?

Dustin.

Dustin who?

**Dustin off my shoes before you
     let me in.**

Knock, knock.

Who's there?

Ari.

Ari who?

**Ari going to tell some more jokes
     today?**

Knock, knock.

Who's there?

Isaac.

Isaac who?

Isaac of knocking so I'm going home!

Knock, knock.

Who's there?

Aldo.

Aldo who?

Aldo anything, if you'll just let me in!

Knock, knock.

Who's there?

Waiter.

Waiter who?

Waiter minute and I'll tell you

    another knock-knock joke!

Knock, knock.

Who's there?

Doug.

Doug who?

I Doug that joke! You got another one?

Knock, knock.

Who's there?

Harrison.

Harrison who?

**Harrison my eyes so I can't see the
doorbell.**

Knock, knock.

Who's there?

Queen.

Queen who?

**Queen your room so we can go out
and play.**

Knock, knock.

Who's there?

Poet.

Poet who?

Poet your money where your mouth is.

Knock, knock.

Who's there?

Winner.

Winner who?

Winner we going to the movies

today?

- - - - - - - - - - - - - - - - - - - -

Knock, knock.

Who's there?

Gideon.

Gideon who?

All Gideon aside, I think you're the best!

Knock, knock.

Who's there?

Carmen.

Carmen who?

I'm Carmen over to tell you another knock-knock joke!

Knock, knock.

Who's there?

Brenda.

Brenda who?

Brenda the guests for the party get here?

Knock, knock.

Who's there?

Abbott.

Abbott who?

I've got an Abbot of biting my nails!

Knock, knock.

Who's there?

Thor.

Thor who?

Thor knuckles after all this knocking!

Knock, knock.

Who's there?

Drew.

Drew who?

Drew you think now is a good time to let me in?

Knock, knock.

Who's there?

Adam.

Adam who?

Adam my way, I'm coming in!

Knock, knock.

Who's there?

Lucy.

Lucy who?

Open up and Lucy who it is!

Knock, knock.

Who's there?

Anita.

Anita who?

Anita hear another knock-knock joke!

Knock, knock.

Who's there?

Mabel.

Mabel who?

Mabel isn't working so you'll have to keep knocking.

Knock, knock.

Who's there?

Raymond.

Raymond who?

**Raymond me to tell you my favorite
knock-knock joke.**

Knock, knock.

Who's there?

Gwen.

Gwen who?

**Gwen do you want to hear another
knock-knock joke?**

Knock, knock.

Who's there?

Ben.

Ben who?

Ben too long since I've come over for a visit!

Knock, knock.

Who's there?

Warren.

Warren who?

I'm Warren out from all this knocking!

Knock, knock.

Who's there?

Say.

Say who?

Who.

Knock, knock.

Who's there?

Russell.

Russell who?

Russell up some grub. I'm hungry!

Knock, knock.

Who's there?

Rex.

Rex who?

I Rex my homework when I leave it out in the rain.

Knock, knock.

Who's there?

Andy.

Andy who?

Andy friend of yours is a friend of mine.

Knock, knock.

Who's there?

Candice.

Candice who?

Candice be the last knock-knock joke?

Knock, knock.

Who's there?

Wade.

Wade who?

Wade any longer, and I'm going to need to sit down!

Knock, knock.

Who's there?

Moe.

Moe who?

Moe jokes, please!

Knock, knock.

Who's there?

Howard.

Howard who?

Howard you like to hear another knock-knock joke?

Knock, knock.

Who's there?

Albion.

Albion who?

Albion time for school this morning.

Knock, knock.

Who's there?

Dennis.

Dennis who?

The Dennis said I have a cavity in my tooth.

Knock, knock.

Who's there?

Thomas.

Thomas who?

**Thomas running out to tell more
knock-knock jokes!**

Knock, knock.

Who's there?

Maxine.

Maxine who?

**Maxine you when you came out and
played.**

Knock, knock.

Who's there?

Emmett.

Emmett who?

Emmett a really nice person at the park today!

Knock, knock.

Who's there?

Astronaut.

Astronaut who?

Astronaut what your country can do for you but what you can do for your country!

Knock, knock.

Who's there?

Frank.

Frank who?

Be Frank. Do you think these jokes
   are funny?

Knock, knock.

Who's there?

Mandy.

Mandy who?

Mandy weather outside is awesome!

Knock, knock.

Who's there?

Justin.

Justin who?

Justin time for another knock-knock joke.

Knock, knock.

Who's there?

Stan.

Stan who?

If I Stan here long enough, will you let me in?

Knock, knock.

Who's there?

Finley.

Finley who?

Finley you came to the door!

Knock, knock.

Who's there?

Ivan.

Ivan who?

Ivan waiting to tell you another knock-knock joke!

Knock, knock.

Who's there?

Ferdie.

Ferdie who?

**Ferdie last time, would you open up
   already?**

Knock, knock.

Who's there?

Eustace.

Eustace who?

Eustace one of my favorite people.

Knock, knock.

Who's there?

Thelma.

Thelma who?

Thelma no secrets, I'll tell you no lies.

Knock, knock.

Who's there?

Florist.

Florist who?

The florist in need of a good sweeping.

Knock, knock.

Who's there?

Henrietta.

Henrietta who?

Henrietta bug, and it made him sick.

Knock, knock.

Who's there?

Noah.

Noah who?

Noah guy who can open the door?

Knock, knock.

Who's there?

Anita.

Anita who?

Anita tell another knock-knock joke before I go!

Knock, knock.

Who's there?

Haddie.

Haddie who?

Haddie great time, so I'll come again soon!

Knock, knock.

Who's there?

Doris.

Doris who?

The Doris stuck so pull harder!

Knock, knock.

Who's there?

Axel.

Axel who?

You Axel lot of questions!

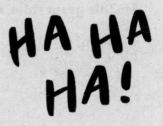

Knock, knock.

Who's there?

Cam.

Cam who?

Cam you come out and play?

Knock, knock.

Who's there?

Paul.

Paul who?

Paul harder and maybe the door will open this time!

Knock, knock.

Who's there?

Misty.

Misty who?

Misty news that I was coming over?

Knock, knock.

Who's there?

Peter.

Peter who?

Peter boots on when it's snowing

outside!

Knock, knock.

Who's there?

Oldest.

Oldest who?

**Oldest laughing is giving me a
bellyache!**

Knock, knock.

Who's there?

Willie.

Willie who?

I'm Willie excited to see you today!

Knock, knock.

Who's there?

Jess.

Jess who?

It's Jess me, so open up!

Knock, knock.

Who's there?

Troy.

Troy who?

**Troy to come up with your own
    knock-knock joke.**

Knock, knock.

Who's there?

Isaiah.

Isaiah who?

Isaiah lot of jokes, don't I?

Knock, knock.

Who's there?

Luke.

Luke who?

Luke out, here I come!

Knock, knock.

Who's there?

Eva.

Eva who?

Eva told you lately that I love you?

Knock, knock.

Who's there?

Sarah.

Sarah who?

Sarah doctor in the house? I'm not feeling well!

Knock, knock.

Who's there?

Wilma.

Wilma who?

Wilma lunch be ready soon?

Knock, knock.

Who's there?

Russian.

Russian who?

I'm Russian around to get ready for school!

Knock, knock.

Who's there?

Wendy.

Wendy who?

Wendy we get to hear another knock-knock joke?

Knock, knock.

Who's there?

Alma.

Alma who?

Alma friends want to meet you!

Knock, knock.

Who's there?

Alex.

Alex who?

**Alex one more time if you're going to
 open up!**

Knock, knock.

Who's there?

Curtis.

Curtis who?

**The Curtis thing to do is to say please
 and thank you.**

Knock, knock.

Who's there?

Ashley.

Ashley who?

Ashley, I would like to tell another knock-knock joke!

Knock, knock.

Who's there?

Sadie.

Sadie who?

Sadie magic word, and I'll come in!

Knock, knock.

Who's there?

Taylor.

Taylor who?

Taylor friends it's time to go to the movies.

Knock, knock.

Who's there?

Anita.

Anita who?

Anita go to the bathroom, so open up!

Knock, knock.

Who's there?

Sam.

Sam who?

Sam day your prince will come!

Knock, knock.

Who's there?

August.

August who?

August you were home, but August

   wrong!

Knock, knock.

Who's there?

Vanessa.

Vanessa who?

Vanessa good time to come out and play?

Knock, knock.

Who's there?

Willy.

Willy who?

I Willy want to tell you another knock-knock joke!

Knock, knock.

Who's there?

Bruce.

Bruce who?

**I'll have Bruce knuckles after all of
    this knocking!**

Knock, knock.

Who's there?

Dwight.

Dwight who?

**The Dwight thing to do is to open the
    door!**

Knock, knock.

Who's there?

Hayden.

Hayden who?

Hayden seek is my favorite game to play!

Knock, knock.

Who's there?

Dewey.

Dewey who?

Dewey have to stop telling knock-knock jokes?

Knock, knock.

Who's there?

William.

William who?

William mind if I tell another knock-knock joke?

Knock, knock.

Who's there?

Colin.

Colin who?

I'm Colin before I come over next time!

Knock, knock.

Who's there?

Karen.

Karen who?

Karen all my joke books over to your house!

Knock, knock.

Who's there?

Bina.

Bina who?

It's Bina really long day, so can you let me in?

Knock, knock.

Who's there?

Alden.

Alden who?

I'm Alden knocking on this door!

Knock, knock.

Who's there?

Lori.

Lori who?

Lori the blinds because the sun is really bright!

Knock, knock.

Who's there?

Cassie.

Cassie who?

Cassie the forest for the trees!

Knock, knock.

Who's there?

Benjamin.

Benjamin who?

Benjamin to the radio all day long!

Knock, knock.

Who's there?

Avery.

Avery who?

Avery time I come over, I have a great time!

Knock, knock.

Who's there?

Rita.

Rita who?

Rita good book lately?

Knock, knock.

Who's there?

Augustus.

Augustus who?

Augustus is the last knock-knock joke for today!

Knock, knock.

Who's there?

Amelia.

Amelia who?

Amelia letter at the post office today.

Knock, knock.

Who's there?

Stan.

Stan who?

I can't Stan waiting for you this long!

Knock, knock.

Who's there?

Betty.

Betty who?

Betty doesn't normally take this long to answer!

Knock, knock.

Who's there?

Emma.

Emma who?

Emma little thirsty. May I have a drink?

Knock, knock.

Who's there?

Author.

Author who?

Author more jokes in store for us?

Knock, knock.

Who's there?

Sherlock.

Sherlock who?

Sherlock the door when you're not home.

Knock, knock.

Who's there?

Judah.

Judah who?

Judah thought someone would have answered by now!

Knock, knock.

Who's there?

Dawn.

Dawn who?

Dawn leave until you hear another knock-knock joke!

Knock, knock.

Who's there?

Ida.

Ida who?

Ida like to hang out with you today!

Knock, knock.

Who's there?

Toran.

Toran who?

**Toran between knocking some more
and just going home!**

Knock, knock.

Who's there?

Amish.

Amish who?

Amish you when we're apart.

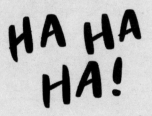

Knock, knock.

Who's there?

Mother.

Mother who?

Mother chance for you to hear a knock-knock joke!

Knock, knock.

Who's there?

Eskimo.

Eskimo who?

Eskimo questions, I'll tell you no lies.

Knock, knock.

Who's there?

Gordon.

Gordon who?

Gordon to the forecast, it's a great

day to play outside!

Knock, knock.

Who's there?

Actor.

Actor who?

Actor age and not your shoe size!

Knock, knock.

Who's there?

Teresa.

Teresa who?

Teresa changing colors so it must be autumn.

Knock, knock.

Who's there?

Usher.

Usher who?

Usher would like to come inside!

Knock, knock.

Who's there?

Alto.

Alto who?

Alto your car to the shop if it needs a

mechanic.

Knock, knock.

Who's there?

Todd.

Todd who?

Todd you this joke book was funny!

Knock, knock.

Who's there?

Sid.

Sid who?

Sid down and let me tell you another knock-knock joke!

Knock, knock.

Who's there?

Watson.

Watson who?

Watson your mind these days?

Knock, knock.

Who's there?

Gladys.

Gladys who?

Gladys time for another knock-knock joke!

Knock, knock.

Who's there?

Jessie.

Jessie who?

Jessie what I got you for your birthday?

Knock, knock.

Who's there?

Violet.

Violet who?

Violet you in on a little secret.

Knock, knock.

Who's there?

Sharon.

Sharon who?

Sharon my candy if you'll let me in!

Knock, knock.

Who's there?

Levi.

Levi who?

Levi key under the mat next time!

Knock, knock.

Who's there?

Max.

Max who?

Max me happy to see you today!

Knock, knock.

Who's there?

Harry.

Harry who?

Harry up and come outside to play!

Knock, knock.

Who's there?

Israeli.

Israeli who?

Israeli cold out here, so open up!

Knock, knock.

Who's there?

Ava.

Ava who?

Ava lot more knock-knock jokes to tell you today!

Knock, knock.

Who's there?

Nolan.

Nolan who?

Nolan you makes me happy!

Knock, knock.

Who's there?

Esther.

Esther who?

Esther another way to get in?

Knock, knock.

Who's there?

Whitney.

Whitney who?

Whitney longer, and I'll lose my patience!

Knock, knock.

Who's there?

Sadie.

Sadie who?

Sadie word and I'll be right over.

Knock, knock.

Who's there?

Alda.

Alda who?

**Alda knocking is giving me a
    headache!**

Knock, knock.

Who's there?

You.

You who?

What? I'm right here!

Knock, knock.

Who's there?

Annie.

Annie who?

Annie friends want to hear another knock-knock joke?

Knock, knock.

Who's there?

Wyatt.

Wyatt who?

Wyatt take you so long to answer the door?

Knock, knock.

Who's there?

Willow.

Willow who?

Willow tell me your favorite joke?

Knock, knock.

Who's there?

Maya.

Maya who?

Maya-rm is really hurting from all this knocking!

Knock, knock.

Who's there?

Soprano.

Soprano who?

I can play some songs on soprano for you if you open up!

Knock, knock.

Who's there?

Sara.

Sara who?

Sara 'nother way to get in?

Knock, knock.

Who's there?

Ash.

Ash who?

Are you catching a cold?

Knock, knock.

Who's there?

Earl.

Earl who?

Earl to bed, Earl to rise.

Knock, knock.

Who's there?

Artist.

Artist who?

Artist came by to say hello.

Knock, knock.

Who's there?

Riley.

Riley who?

Riley think you should let me in soon!

Knock, knock.

Who's there?

Sally.

Sally who?

Sally goose, it's just me.

Knock, knock.

Who's there?

Brad.

Brad who?

Brad news: I can tell you only one joke today.

Knock, knock.

Who's there?

Nathan.

Nathan who?

Nathan like a funny joke to make you smile.

Knock, knock.

Who's there?

Pastor.

Pastor who?

Pastor bedtime, so go to sleep!

Knock, knock.

Who's there?

Becca.

Becca who?

Becca way from the door. I'm

coming in!

Knock, knock.

Who's there?

Benny.

Benny who?

Benny long time since I came over!

Knock, knock.

Who's there?

Humphrey.

Humphrey who?

**Humphrey to come over if you want
to hang out.**

Knock, knock.

Who's there?

Micah.

Micah who?

Micah me an offer I can't refuse!

Knock, knock.

Who's there?

Martian.

Martian who?

**I'm martian to the beat of my own
    drum!**

Knock, knock.

Who's there?

Darrell.

Darrell who?

**Darrell be some consequences if you
   don't open up!**

Knock, knock.

Who's there?

Weirdo.

Weirdo who?

Weirdo you want to go for lunch?

Knock, knock.

Who's there?

Nate.

Nate who?

Better Nate than never.

Knock, knock.

Who's there?

Eileen.

Eileen who?

Eileen over to tie my shoes.

Knock, knock.

Who's there?

Norman.

Norman who?

Norman likes a party pooper.

Knock, knock.

Who's there?

Howie.

Howie who?

Howie going to go to the movies if you don't open up?

Knock, knock.

Who's there?

Grayson.

Grayson who?

Grayson you with my presence today.

Knock, knock.

Who's there?

Jester.

Jester who?

You're Jester time to hear another knock-knock joke!

Knock, knock.

Who's there?

Ferris.

Ferris who?

**Ferris and elves are just make-
      believe.**

Knock, knock.

Who's there?

Albert.

Albert who?

Albert you never guess!

Knock, knock.

Who's there?

Lucas.

Lucas who?

Lucas in the eyes and tell us the truth!

Knock, knock.

Who's there?

Isabel.

Isabel who?

Isabel ringing on your phone?

HA HA HA!

Knock, knock.

Who's there?

Alexia.

Alexia who?

Alexia one more time to open the door.

Knock, knock.

Who's there?

Mia.

Mia who?

Mia favorite thing to do is tell knock-knock jokes!

Knock, knock.

Who's there?

Tenor.

Tenor who?

Tenor eleven more jokes and we'll be finished.

Knock, knock.

Who's there?

Girlie.

Girlie who?

Girlie to bed, early to rise.

Knock, knock.

Who's there?

Summer.

Summer who?

Summer fast at opening the door and summer not!

Knock, knock.

Who's there?

Clara.

Clara who?

Clara place at the dinner table for me.

Knock, knock.

Who's there?

Charlotte.

Charlotte who?

Charlotte of things to like about you!

Things

Knock, knock.

Who's there?

Fleas.

Fleas who?

Fleas a jolly good fellow!

Knock, knock.

Who's there?

Pig.

Pig who?

Pig up the pace and open the door!

Knock, knock.

Who's there?

Denture.

Denture who?

Denture think it's about time for another knock-knock joke?

Knock, knock.

Who's there?

Cauliflower.

Cauliflower who?

Cauliflower by any other name, and it will smell as sweet.

Knock, knock.

Who's there?

Poetry.

Poetry who?

Poetry in the backyard for some shade.

Knock, knock.

Who's there?

Wander.

Wander who?

Wander if you'll ever open the door!

Knock, knock.

Who's there?

Walnut.

Walnut who?

Walnut open the door so I can tell you another knock-knock joke?

Knock, knock.

Who's there?

Tickle.

Tickle who?

A tickle bite your dog!

Knock, knock.

Who's there?

Llama.

Llama who?

Llama know if you want to hear
another knock-knock joke.

Knock, knock.

Who's there?

Wing.

Wing who?

Wing do you think you'll be able to let
me inside?

Knock, knock.

Who's there?

Mouse.

Mouse who?

Mouse I keep knocking all day long?

Knock, knock.

Who's there?

Navy bean.

Navy bean who?

I've navy bean to your house before.

Knock, knock.

Who's there?

Odyssey.

Odyssey who?

Odyssey any reason to stop telling knock-knock jokes!

Knock, knock.

Who's there?

Melon.

Melon who?

You're one in a melon!

Knock, knock.

Who's there?

Waffle.

Waffle who?

I'm waffle glad I could see you today.

Knock, knock.

Who's there?

Money.

Money who?

Money is sore from running all day.

Knock, knock.

Who's there?

Weasel.

Weasel who?

Weasel be late if you don't hurry up!

Knock, knock.

Who's there?

Cashew.

Cashew who?

I cashew reading my joke book today!

Knock, knock.

Who's there?

Toad.

Toad who?

Toad my mom I'd be home for dinner.

Knock, knock.

Who's there?

Needle.

Needle who?

Needle little more time to answer the door?

Knock, knock.

Who's there?

Meow.

Meow who?

Take meow to the ball game!

Knock, knock.

Who's there?

Goatee.

Goatee who?

Goatee the door and find out!

Knock, knock.

Who's there?

Ice cream.

Ice cream who?

Ice cream if you don't let me in!

Knock, knock.

Who's there?

Oyster.

Oyster who?

Oyster marshmallows into my hot cocoa.

Knock, knock.

Who's there?

Grass.

Grass who?

I already know it's you, though.

•

Knock, knock.

Who's there?

Wishing well.

Wishing well who?

**I'm wishing well be together
sometime soon.**

Knock, knock.

Who's there?

Muffin.

Muffin who?

Muffin to do today so let's go have some fun!

Knock, knock.

Who's there?

Mixture.

Mixture who?

I mixture phone call, but I'm here now!

Knock, knock.

Who's there?

Possum.

Possum who?

Possum more snacks over here. I'm hungry!

Knock, knock.

Who's there?

Hives.

Hives who?

Hives been waiting to see you all day!

Knock, knock.

Who's there?

Cod.

Cod who?

Cod you tell me a funny joke?

Knock, knock.

Who's there?

Tomatoes.

Tomatoes who?

I look great from my head tomatoes!

Knock, knock.

Who's there?

Brie.

Brie who?

Don't worry, brie happy!

Knock, knock.

Who's there?

Sofa.

Sofa who?

Sofa these knock-knock jokes are pretty funny!

Knock, knock.

Who's there?

Latin.

Latin who?

Latin you in on a little secret!

Knock, knock.

Who's there?

Apple.

Apple who?

Apple on the doorknob, but it still won't open!

Knock, knock.

Who's there?

Shaver.

Shaver who?

Shaver pennies for a rainy day.

Knock, knock.

Who's there?

Taco.

Taco who?

Let's taco 'bout how we're going to have fun today!

Knock, knock.

Who's there?

Cheetos.

Cheetos who?

Cheetos never win.

Knock, knock.

Who's there?

Sushi.

Sushi who?

Sushi the latest movie at the theater?

Knock, knock.

Who's there?

Blue.

Blue who?

Don't cry. It's just a knock-knock joke!

Knock, knock.

Who's there?

Canoe.

Canoe who?

Canoe tell me your favorite joke today?

Knock, knock.

Who's there?

Bacon.

Bacon who?

I'm bacon you a cake for your birthday!

Knock, knock.

Who's there?

Cereal.

Cereal who?

Cereal pleasure to make your acquaintance!

Knock, knock.

Who's there?

House.

House who?

House about we go to the movies?

Knock, knock.

Who's there?

Wind.

Wind who?

Wind do we get to have a snack?

Knock, knock.

Who's there?

Ignore.

Ignore who?

Knock, knock.

Who's there?

Armageddon.

Armageddon who?

Armageddon really sick of knocking!

Knock, knock.

Who's there?

Treble.

Treble who?

**Treble is heading your way if you
forget your homework!**

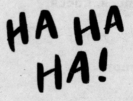

Knock, knock.

Who's there?

Pupil.

Pupil who?

Pupil like to hear a good knock-knock joke!

Knock, knock.

Who's there?

Tennis.

Tennis who?

Tennis how many cents are in a dime.

Knock, knock.

Who's there?

S'more.

S'more who?

S'more jokes would get this party started!

Knock, knock.

Who's there?

Fungi.

Fungi who?

A fungi is ready to tell you another joke!

Knock, knock.

Who's there?

Dragon.

Dragon who?

Quit dragon your feet and open the door!

Knock, knock.

Who's there?

Nutella.

Nutella who?

Nutella what might happen if you open the door!

Knock, knock.

Who's there?

Oxen.

Oxen who?

**Oxen you one more time to answer
the door!**

Knock, knock.

Who's there?

Owls.

Owls who?

And cows moo. What's your point?

Knock, knock.

Who's there?

Costume.

Costume who?

It costume a lot of money to fix his bike!

Knock, knock.

Who's there?

Yam.

Yam who?

Yam so glad to see you today!

Knock, knock.

Who's there?

Road.

Road who?

Road you a letter, but I didn't get a reply!

Knock, knock.

Who's there?

Orange juice.

Orange juice who?

Orange juice going to look out the window and see who it is?

Knock, knock.

Who's there?

Livid.

Livid who?

If you livid closer, I would visit more often!

Knock, knock.

Who's there?

Lemon.

Lemon who?

Lemon know when you're ready to play with me!

Knock, knock.

Who's there?

Beaver.

Beaver who?

Beaver I go, I should tell you one more knock-knock joke!

Knock, knock.

Who's there?

Olive oil.

Olive oil who?

Olive oil in my car to keep it running.

Knock, knock.

Who's there?

Myth.

Myth who?

I myth you, too, so let's get together!

Knock, knock.

Who's there?

Gorilla.

Gorilla who?

Gorilla me a steak—I'm hungry!

Knock, knock.

Who's there?

Sardine.

Sardine who?

I'm sardine to think you're never

   going to open this door!

Knock, knock.

Who's there?

Auto.

Auto who?

You auto come out and play with me!

Knock, knock.

Who's there?

Itch.

Itch who?

Bless you!

Knock, knock.

Who's there?

Zinc.

Zinc who?

Zinc about going on a picnic with me.

Knock, knock.

Who's there?

Wheel.

Wheel who?

**Wheel both have a lot more fun when
you let me in!**

Knock, knock.

Who's there?

Ostrich.

Ostrich who?

**If ostrich, I could buy you an
expensive present!**

Knock, knock.

Who's there?

Collie.

Collie who?

Collie friend when you need a hug.

Knock, knock.

Who's there?

Gas.

Gas who?

Gas who? I already know it's you!

Knock, knock.

Who's there?

Beehive.

Beehive who?

Beehive at the store, or you won't get any candy!

Knock, knock.

Who's there?

Puddle.

Puddle who?

Puddle little muscle into it!

Knock, knock.

Who's there?

Udder.

Udder who?

Udder than me, who tells a great joke?

Knock, knock.

Who's there?

Toucan.

Toucan who?

Toucan play at this game!

Knock, knock.

Who's there?

Petunia.

Petunia who?

Petunia shoes and come outside!

Knock, knock.

Who's there?

Moose.

Moose who?

Moose you take so long to answer the

   door?

Knock, knock.

Who's there?

Yolk.

Yolk who?

The yolk's on you!

Knock, knock.

Who's there?

Gopher.

Gopher who?

**Gopher a ride around the block
with me?**

Knock, knock.

Who's there?

Roach.

Roach who?

I roach you a letter to let you know I was coming!

Knock, knock.

Who's there?

Orange.

Orange who?

Orange you glad we have more knock-knock jokes?

Knock, knock.

Who's there?

Tire.

Tire who?

**Tire shoes, or you'll trip when you're
    running!**

Knock, knock.

Who's there?

Godiva.

Godiva who?

Godiva into the deep end of the pool.

Knock, knock.

Who's there?

Worm.

Worm who?

**Worm up your vocal chords and sing
me a song!**

Knock, knock.

Who's there?

Defense.

Defense who?

**Defense is broken, but the gate works
fine!**

Knock, knock.

Who's there?

Ya.

Ya who?

I'm excited to see you, too!

Knock, knock.

Who's there?

Parmesan.

Parmesan who?

A parmesan slip is required for the field trip.

Knock, knock.

Who's there?

Artisan.

Artisan who?

Artisan awesome way to express yourself.

Knock, knock.

Who's there?

Pooch.

Pooch who?

Pooch your arms around me and give me a hug.

Knock, knock.

Who's there?

Ooze.

Ooze who?

Ooze asking the questions here?

Knock, knock.

Who's there?

Carrot.

Carrot who?

You carrot all that I'm standing here waiting for you?

Knock, knock.

Who's there?

Goblin.

Goblin who?

Goblin up my dinner and then I can play!

Knock, knock.

Who's there?

Nacho.

Nacho who?

Nacho turn to tell the jokes this time.

Knock, knock.

Who's there?

Avocado.

Avocado who?

Avocado about three more knock-knock jokes!

Knock, knock.

Who's there?

Wheelbarrow.

Wheelbarrow who?

Wheelbarrow a ball so we can shoot hoops.

Knock, knock.

Who's there?

Hutch.

Hutch who?

Sounds like you're catching a cold!

Knock, knock.

Who's there?

Alien.

Alien who?

Do you know a lot of aliens?

HA HA HA!

Knock, knock.

Who's there?

Water.

Water who?

Water we going to do when we run out of jokes to tell?

Knock, knock.

Who's there?

Mustard.

Mustard who?

It mustard when you stub your toe!

Knock, knock.

Who's there?

Funnel.

Funnel who?

The funnel begin once you open the door!

Knock, knock.

Who's there?

Poodle.

Poodle who?

Poodle little more energy into getting to the door!

Knock, knock.

Who's there?

Wire.

Wire who?

Wire you taking so long to answer the door?

Knock, knock.

Who's there?

Pitcher.

Pitcher who?

Pitcher back into it!

Knock, knock.

Who's there?

Loaf.

Loaf who?

I loaf telling jokes with you!

Knock, knock.

Who's there?

Potty.

Potty who?

**Potty the reason I came over was to
see you. Open up!**

Knock, knock.

Who's there?

Moth.

Moth who?

Moth thumb got shut in the door.

    Ouch!

Knock, knock.

Who's there?

Dingo.

Dingo who?

Dingo away because I want to tell you

    another knock-knock joke.

Knock, knock.

Who's there?

Distress.

Distress who?

Distress is the perfect thing to wear today.

Knock, knock.

Who's there?

Caribou.

Caribou who?

I caribou you because we're friends!

Knock, knock.

Who's there?

Wooden shoe.

Wooden shoe who?

Wooden shoe like to hear me tell another knock-knock joke?

Knock, knock.

Who's there?

Juicy.

Juicy who?

Juicy anything good to eat in the kitchen?

Knock, knock.

Who's there?

Radio.

Radio who?

Radio not, I'm coming in!

Knock, knock.

Who's there?

Cannoli.

Cannoli who?

I cannoli stay for a little while!

Knock, knock.

Who's there?

Queso.

Queso who?

**In queso emergency, where should
I go?**

Knock, knock.

Who's there?

Cactus.

Cactus who?

Cactus makes perfect.

Knock, knock.

Who's there?

Dishes.

Dishes who?

Dishes a great day to hang out together!

Knock, knock.

Who's there?

Howl.

Howl who?

Howl I tell you another knock-knock joke if you don't open up?

Knock, knock.

Who's there?

Herd.

Herd who?

Herd you were in town, so I came right over!

Knock, knock.

Who's there?

Diesel.

Diesel who?

Diesel be a great day!

Knock, knock.

Who's there?

Target.

Target who?

Target a laugh, tell a joke!

Knock, knock.

Who's there?

Square.

Square who?

Square are we going shopping today?

Knock, knock.

Who's there?

Pecan.

Pecan who?

Pecan somebody your own size!

Knock, knock.

Who's there?

Panther.

Panther who?

If your panther falling down, wear a belt!

Knock, knock.

Who's there?

Boil.

Boil who?

Boil you get it if you forget your homework!

Knock, knock.

Who's there?

Igloo.

Igloo who?

Igloo a stamp on the envelope before I mail it.

Knock, knock.

Who's there?

Razor.

Razor who?

Razor hand if you want to hear

another knock-knock joke.

Knock, knock.

Who's there?

Cheese.

Cheese who?

Cheese, it's taking you forever to

answer the door!

Knock, knock.

Who's there?

Iced tea.

Iced tea who?

Iced tea you're ready to come out and

    play with me!

Knock, knock.

Who's there?

Jell-O.

Jell-O who?

Jell-O, I'm happy to see you!

Knock, knock.

Who's there?

Falafel.

Falafel who?

I falafel, so I need to call the doctor.

Knock, knock.

Who's there?

I am.

I am who?

I'm sorry, do you have amnesia?

Knock, knock.

Who's there?

Defeat.

Defeat who?

Defeat are really sore, so can I come in and sit down?

Knock, knock.

Who's there?

Pencil.

Pencil who?

His pencil fall down if he doesn't wear suspenders!

LOL!

Knock, knock.

Who's there?

Ostrich.

Ostrich who?

Ostrich before I go for a run.

Knock, knock.

Who's there?

Donut.

Donut who?

Donut you love a good knock-knock joke?

Knock, knock.

Who's there?

Camouflage.

Camouflage who?

Camouflage, or is the toilet broken?

Knock, knock.

Who's there?

Claws.

Claws who?

**Claws the door behind you, or you'll
    let the dog out!**

Knock, knock.

Who's there?

Disguise.

Disguise who?

Disguise getting on my nerves!

Knock, knock.

Who's there?

Axe.

Axe who?

Axe me a silly question, you'll get a silly answer.

Knock, knock.

Who's there?

Rhino.

Rhino who?

Rhino you want to hear another knock-knock joke?

Knock, knock.

Who's there?

Fairy.

Fairy who?

I'm fairy happy to see you!

- - - - - - - - - - - - - - - - - - - -

Knock, knock.

Who's there?

Gelatin.

Gelatin who?

Gelatin me in or not?

Knock, knock.

Who's there?

Cock-a-doodle.

Cock-a-doodle who?

No, roosters say cock-a-doodle-doo!

Knock, knock.

Who's there?

Fitness.

Fitness who?

Fitness whole pizza in my mouth!

Knock, knock.

Who's there?

Voodoo.

Voodoo who?

Voodoo you want to invite to your birthday party?

Knock, knock.

Who's there?

Stopwatch.

Stopwatch who?

Stopwatch you're doing and let me in!

Knock, knock.

Who's there?

Launch.

Launch who?

Launch is my favorite meal of the day.

Knock, knock.

Who's there?

Chicken.

Chicken who?

Chicken to see if you're ready to come
out and play.

Knock, knock.

Who's there?

Fleece.

Fleece who?

Fleece will make my dog super itchy.

Knock, knock.

Who's there?

Mister.

Mister who?

Mister face so I came to see you!

Knock, knock.

Who's there?

Pool.

Pool who?

Pool open the door and let me in!

Knock, knock.

Who's there?

Tail.

Tail who?

Tail me when it's time for dinner!

Knock, knock.

Who's there?

Amateur.

Amateur who?

Amateur to see you if I come again

   tomorrow?

Knock, knock.

Who's there?

Crab.

Crab who?

Crab your coat and come outside!

Knock, knock.

Who's there?

Field.

Field who?

I field to tell you that I was coming over today!

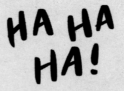

Knock, knock.

Who's there?

Pigeon.

Pigeon who?

Pigeon and help with the dishes!

Knock, knock.

Who's there?

Harmony.

Harmony who?

Harmony times can I tell you a joke?

Knock, knock.

Who's there?

Turnip.

Turnip who?

Turnip the radio—I love this song!

Knock, knock.

Who's there?

Ear.

Ear who?

Ear we go again!

Knock, knock.

Who's there?

Ghost.

Ghost who?

Ghost tell your friends a knock-knock joke!

Knock, knock.

Who's there?

Mule.

Mule who?

Mule be glad you answered the door!

Knock, knock.

Who's there?

Thistle.

Thistle who?

Thistle be the best knock-knock joke yet!

Knock, knock.

Who's there?

Omelet.

Omelet who?

Omelet smarter than you think I am!

Knock, knock.

Who's there?

Donkey.

Donkey who?

My donkey won't unlock this door!

Knock, knock.

Who's there?

Koala.

Koala who?

Koala me when you're ready to hang out.

Knock, knock.

Who's there?

Forty.

Forty who?

Forty last time, open up!

Knock, knock.

Who's there?

Yeast.

Yeast who?

At yeast we never run out of jokes to

tell!

Knock, knock.

Who's there?

Dozen.

Dozen who?

Dozen anybody want to come out and play?

Knock, knock.

Who's there?

Squid.

Squid who?

Squid stalling and open up!

Knock, knock.

Who's there?

Butter.

Butter who?

Butter not run out of knock-knock jokes!

Knock, knock.

Who's there?

Peas.

Peas who?

Peas and thank you are good manners.

Knock, knock.

Who's there?

Pasta.

Pasta who?

I pasta test with flying colors!

Knock, knock.

Who's there?

Soup.

Soup who?

It's soup to you if I tell another knock-

   knock joke!

Knock, knock.

Who's there?

Leash.

Leash who?

The leash you could do is open the door!

Knock, knock.

Who's there?

Howdy.

Howdy who?

Howdy come up with all these knock-knock jokes?

Places

Knock, knock.

Who's there?

Alaska.

Alaska who?

Alaska one more time if you can come out and play!

Knock, knock.

Who's there?

Pasture.

Pasture who?

Pasture house, so I thought I'd stop by.

Knock, knock.

Who's there?

Nevada.

Nevada who?

It's Nevada best idea to tell a lie.

Knock, knock.

Who's there?

Dallas.

Dallas who?

Dallas time I told you a joke, you laughed out loud.

Knock, knock.

Who's there?

Denmark.

Denmark who?

Denmark up my joke book with your pencil!

Knock, knock.

Who's there?

Everest.

Everest who?

Do you Everest from reading these knock-knock jokes?

Knock, knock.

Who's there?

Heaven.

Heaven who?

Heaven a great time telling these knock-knock jokes!

Knock, knock.

Who's there?

Dubai.

Dubai who?

Dubai me a present for my birthday?

Knock, knock.

Who's there?

Tokyo.

Tokyo who?

**Tokyo long enough to answer the
door!**

Knock, knock.

Who's there?

Augusta.

Augusta who?

**Augusta wind blew away my
homework!**

Knock, knock.

Who's there?

Warsaw.

Warsaw who?

I'm Warsaw than I thought!

Knock, knock.

Who's there?

Czech.

Czech who?

**Czech and see if you can come out
and play!**

Knock, knock.

Who's there?

Sweden.

Sweden who?

I'll Sweden my oatmeal with some sugar.

Knock, knock.

Who's there?

Aspen.

Aspen who?

Aspen all day telling knock-knock jokes.

Knock, knock.

Who's there?

Safari.

Safari who?

Safari like these knock-knock jokes!

Knock, knock.

Who's there?

Cairo.

Cairo who?

I Cairo 'bout your feelings.

Knock, knock.

Who's there?

Alley.

Alley who?

Alley want to do is hang out with you
    today.

Knock, knock.

Who's there?

Tibet.

Tibet who?

Tibet we can't just tell jokes all day
    long.

Knock, knock.

Who's there?

Kenya.

Kenya who?

Kenya tell me one more knock-knock joke?

Knock, knock.

Who's there?

Aloe.

Aloe who?

No, in Hawaii it's "Aloha!"

Knock, knock.

Who's there?

Iran.

Iran who?

**Iran all the way here, so I need a
  break!**

Knock, knock.

Who's there?

Dublin.

Dublin who?

**I'm Dublin how many cookies I bake
  tomorrow.**

Knock, knock.

Who's there?

Kentucky.

Kentucky who?

I Kentucky myself into bed.

Knock, knock.

Who's there?

France.

France who?

True France should stick together!

Knock, knock.

Who's there?

Florida.

Florida who?

Florida last time, open the door!

Knock, knock.

Who's there?

Europe.

Europe who?

Europe early this morning.

Knock, knock.

Who's there?

Congo.

Congo who?

I Congo to the movies with you!

Knock, knock.

Who's there?

Hawaii.

Hawaii who?

Hawaii doing? I'm feeling great!

Knock, knock.

Who's there?

Juneau.

Juneau who?

Juneau any good knock-knock jokes?

Knock, knock.

Who's there?

Planet.

Planet who?

I'll planet to see you again tomorrow.

Knock, knock.

Who's there?

Eden.

Eden who?

Eden dessert after I finish my dinner.

Knock, knock.

Who's there?

Norway.

Norway who?

Norway am I going to stop telling knock-knock jokes!

Knock, knock.

Who's there?

Venice.

Venice who?

Venice dinner going to be ready?

Knock, knock.

Who's there?

Atlas.

Atlas who?

Atlas I can tell you another knock-knock joke!

HA HA HA!

Knock, knock.

Who's there?

Oslo.

Oslo who?

Oslo to finish my chores today.

Knock, knock.

Who's there?

Jamaica.

Jamaica who?

Jamaica me want to tell you another knock-knock joke!

Knock, knock.

Who's there?

Shore.

Shore who?

Shore would love to hang out with you today!

Knock, knock.

Who's there?

Yukon.

Yukon who?

Yukon try to beat me in a game of checkers today!

Knock, knock.

Who's there?

Russia.

Russia who?

Russia little faster or you'll be late!

Knock, knock.

Who's there?

Avenue.

Avenue who?

Avenue heard enough knock-knock jokes yet?

Knock, knock.

Who's there?

Uganda.

Uganda who?

Uganda go to the playground

with me?

Knock, knock.

Who's there?

Ireland.

Ireland who?

If Ireland you my soccer ball, will you

bring it back?

Knock, knock.

Who's there?

Havana.

Havana who?

Havana a great time with you today!

Knock, knock.

Who's there?

Italy.

Italy who?

Italy a sad day if we run out of knock-knock jokes!

Knock, knock.

Who's there?

Amarillo.

Amarillo who?

**Amarillo nice person once you get to
know me!**

Knock, knock.

Who's there?

Alabama.

Alabama who?

**Alabama on the door until you
open up!**

Knock, knock.

Who's there?

Jupiter.

Jupiter who?

Jupiter foot in your mouth that time!

Holiday/Seasonal

Knock, knock.

Who's there?

Snow.

Snow who?

Snow way will I stop telling knock-knock jokes!

Knock, knock.

Who's there?

Winter.

Winter who?

Winter the store to buy some hot chocolate.

Knock, knock.

Who's there?

Iris.

Iris who?

Iris you a Happy Hanukkah!

Knock, knock.

Who's there?

Allies.

Allies who?

**Allies want for Christmas is my two
front teeth!**

Knock, knock.

Who's there?

Ada.

Ada who?

Ada dozen Christmas cookies, and
   now I feel sick!

Knock, knock.

Who's there?

Butcher.

Butcher who?

Butcher Christmas presents under
   the tree.

Knock, knock.

Who's there?

Handsome.

Handsome who?

Handsome of that Halloween candy to me!

Knock, knock.

Who's there?

Glove.

Glove who?

Glove playing in the snow in the winter!

Knock, knock.

Who's there?

Window.

Window who?

Window we go hunting for Easter eggs?

Knock, knock.

Who's there?

Dante.

Dante who?

Dante want to go trick-or-treating with us?

Knock, knock.

Who's there?

Gary.

Gary who?

Gary the treats to the Christmas party!

Knock, knock.

Who's there?

Ruby.

Ruby who?

Ruby sure to come to my birthday party.

Knock, knock.

Who's there?

Sleigh.

Sleigh who?

Sleigh you'll give me a Christmas present!

Knock, knock.

Who's there?

Woolly.

Woolly who?

Woolly really come down the chimney on Christmas Eve?

Knock, knock.

Who's there?

Elephant.

Elephant who?

Elephant for Thanksgiving dinner is a piece of pumpkin pie.

Knock, knock.

Who's there?

Winnebago.

Winnebago who?

Winnebago candy at the Halloween party!

Knock, knock.

Who's there?

Esther.

Esther who?

**Esther going to be fireworks on the
Fourth of July?**

Knock, knock.

Who's there?

Murray.

Murray who?

**Murray Christmas and Happy New
Year!**

Knock, knock.

Who's there?

Dizzy.

Dizzy who?

Dizzy the best holiday of the year.

Knock, knock.

Who's there?

Elf.

Elf who?

Elf finish decorating the Christmas tree tomorrow!

Knock, knock.

Who's there?

Waldo.

Waldo who?

Waldo we wear for Halloween this year?

Knock, knock.

Who's there?

Marion.

Marion who?

May your Christmas be Marion bright!

Knock, knock.

Who's there?

Snowshoes.

Snowshoes who?

Snowshoes, no shirt: no service!

Knock, knock.

Who's there?

Candy.

Candy who?

Candy kids go trick-or-treating together?

Knock, knock.

Who's there?

Rabbit.

Rabbit who?

Rabbit quick and put it under the Christmas tree!

Knock, knock.

Who's there?

Tommy.

Tommy who?

Tommy hurts from eating too much Halloween candy!

Knock, knock.

Who's there?

Pudding.

Pudding who?

Pudding my eggs in the Easter basket.

Knock, knock.

Who's there?

Arthur.

Arthur who?

Arthur any more Christmas presents to open?

Knock, knock.

Who's there?

Carolyn.

Carolyn who?

Carolyn spreads Christmas cheer.

Knock, knock.

Who's there?

Cherise.

Cherise who?

**Cherise fun to celebrate the holidays
with you!**

Knock, knock.

Who's there?

Tree.

Tree who?

Tree wise men followed the star!

Knock, knock.

Who's there?

Abby.

Abby who?

Abby birthday to you!

Knock, knock.

Who's there?

Santa Claus.

Santa Claus who?

You don't know who Santa Claus is?!

Knock, knock.

Who's there?

Sandy.

Sandy who?

Sandy Claus is coming to town!

Knock, knock.

Who's there?

Kari.

Kari who?

Kari my valentines to the party, please?

Knock, knock.

Who's there?

Lucas.

Lucas who?

Lucas time to open our Christmas presents!

Knock, knock.

Who's there?

Fishy.

Fishy who?

I fishy would be my valentine!

Knock, knock.

Who's there?

Snowman.

Snowman who?

Snowman would turn down a

    Christmas present!

Knock, knock.

Who's there.

Frostbite.

Frostbite who?

Frostbite your food and then chew it.

Knock, knock.

Who's there?

Sofa.

Sofa who?

Sofa this is the best holiday ever!

Knock, knock.

Who's there?

Lena.

Lena who?

Lena little closer, and I'll tell you
who's my valentine.

Knock, knock.

Who's there?

Ellie.

Ellie who?

Ellie want is to be your valentine!

HA HA HA!

Knock, knock.

Who's there?

Freeze.

Freeze who?

Freeze a jolly good fellow!

Knock, knock.

Who's there?

Minnow.

Minnow who?

Let minnow when you're ready to go trick-or-treating!

Knock, knock.

Who's there?

Needle.

Needle who?

Needle little more icing for my

 Christmas cookies!

Knock, knock.

Who's there?

Mushroom.

Mushroom who?

Not mushroom for more presents

 under the tree!

Knock, knock.

Who's there?

Pizza.

Pizza who?

Pizza earth, goodwill to men.

Knock, knock.

Who's there?

Iguana.

Iguana who?

Iguana big piece of pie at

    Thanksgiving!

Knock, knock.

Who's there?

Darrel.

Darrel who?

**Darrel be lots of friends at the party
today.**

Knock, knock.

Who's there?

Wanda.

Wanda who?

Wanda be my valentine?

Knock, knock.

Who's there?

Iris.

Iris who?

Iris you a Merry Christmas!

Knock, knock.

Who's there?

Stella.

Stella who?

Stella lot of ornaments to hang on the tree.

Knock, knock.

Who's there?

Rooster.

Rooster who?

Rooster turkey for Thanksgiving dinner!

Knock, knock.

Who's there?

Alpaca.

Alpaca who?

Alpaca watermelon for our Fourth of July picnic.

Knock, knock.

Who's there?

Mustache.

Mustache who?

Mustache if you're done with your Christmas shopping!

Knock, knock.

Who's there?

Feline.

Feline who?

Feline better since you said you'd be my Valentine!

Knock, knock.

Who's there?

Milton.

Milton who?

Milton snow means no more sledding.

Knock, knock.

Who's there?

Welcome.

Welcome who?

Welcome trick-or-treating with you!

Knock, knock.

Who's there?

Water.

Water who?

Water you doing on New Year's Eve?

Knock, knock.

Who's there?

Aloe vera.

Aloe vera who?

Aloe vera much! Will you be my Valentine?

Knock, knock.

Who's there?

Yacht.

Yacht who?

Yacht to open your present and see

what you got for your birthday!

Knock, knock.

Who's there?

Waddle.

Waddle who?

Waddle we do if we don't find all the

Easter eggs?